Unwritten: The Poems That Never Were

Jerald Infant Jeyarethinam

BookLeaf Publishing

India | USA | UK

Presentation by *BookLeaf Publishing*

Web: www.bookleafpub.com

E-mail: info@bookleafpub.com

ISBN: 9789360949198

First edition 2024

DEDICATION

To those who left and those who stayed.

ACKNOWLEDGEMENT

As I pen these acknowledgments for "Unwritten: The Poems That Never Were," I am reminded of the tumultuous yet transformative journey that has led me to this moment. The last few years have been nothing short of life-altering in the truest sense. Facing situations beyond my wildest imaginings, I've come to a stark realization: my path here was paved with my own choices and mistakes.

It would be easy to attribute my missteps to a lack of love, but that would be far from the truth. Grief, loss, betrayal – these are experiences that undoubtedly shape us, but through it all, love has remained a constant, albeit sometimes overshadowed by other emotions. Love, I've learned, is what keeps me anchored in life, even when storms rage within.

I once fancied myself invulnerable, but reality delivered a sobering blow, shattering this illusion. There's no 'undo' button in life, a lesson I learned the hard way, despite the universe's repeated warnings and the guidance of my heart, which I too often ignored.

In grappling with the concept of death, I realized my fear wasn't of dying, but of dying empty, without having given back to those who have enriched my life. My faith wavered in the wake of personal losses, and I struggled with the feeling of being disconnected from God, from my inner self.

In these times of trial, I discovered invaluable support in the form of people and situations that guided me step by uncertain step. My family and my friends have been unwavering in their belief in me, their pain at my suffering a constant reminder of the love that surrounds me.

This book, a culmination of my experiences and reflections, is also a testament to the unyielding support I've received. It's a tribute to the resilience of the human spirit and the power of love and faith to guide us back to ourselves. To those who stood by me, who believe in a brighter tomorrow for me: thank you. Your faith fuels my journey towards rediscovery and fulfillment.

As I continue to navigate through the remnants of past fears and pains, I am bolstered by the knowledge that I am not alone. There is still a purpose for me to fulfill, and each day is an opportunity to inch closer to it. With renewed determination and hope, I embrace the path ahead, ever grateful for the love and guidance that light my way.

PREFACE

Is it true that every story, whether rooted in reality or woven from the threads of imagination, must find its way to an end? This is a notion that has long been ingrained in our understanding of narratives, but I find myself questioning its veracity. Perhaps the concept of an ending is merely another construct, a boundary artificially imposed upon us like so many others.

From the moment of the universe's inexplicable leap from nothingness into being, a story began – a story still being etched across the vast, cosmic canvas in a state of perpetual and glorious chaos. This grand narrative, with its unseeable conclusion, envelops us all, making us but characters in an epic far greater than any we could conceive.

In "Unwritten: The Poems That Never Were," I explore this concept – that our lives are composed of such unfinished tales. Each of us carries a collection of narratives, fragmented and incomplete, that intersect with the lives of others. These intersections, these fleeting moments of connection, contribute to the ever-expanding chaos of existence. Our stories, with their abrupt leaps and unexpected turns, defy the conventional structure and predictable closure.

This book is a reflection on these unfinished stories, an homage to the beauty of the unresolved and the unexpressed. It's an invitation to ponder the fluidity of our narratives and the possibility that, in the grand scheme of things, there are no true endings, only pauses, before the next chapter begins.

As you delve into these pages, I encourage you to embrace the chaos of your own story, to find peace in its lack of conclusion, and to celebrate the beauty in the stories left unwritten. For it is in these spaces – the gaps between what is said and what is left unsaid – that the true poetry of life resides.

Contents

Act I: Love and Hope

Finders Keepers

In the shroud of wilderness, unseen,
forgot,
It gave all it had, every fervent thought.

Longing to share a song, a melody bright,
Yearning for voice in the stillness of night.

This void was more than an empty space,
More than a hollow, forgotten place.

Here once dwelled a heart, alive and free,
Glowing with passion, unbound and fiery.

Death, in its cold grasp, could never seize,
The wild, untamed spirit of a heart at
ease.

Caged, it languished, a creature so wild,
In dust and dreams, forever beguiled.

Burdens of dreams, heavy as stone,
Fading beats in a rhythm unknown.

It sought escape, a path obscure,
Into the darkness, without a cure.

Then, in austerity's solemn embrace,
A symbol of hope with a floral grace.

With a bloom adorning her brow,
She rescued the heart, here and now.

Revived, my heart beats anew,
Guarded and cherished, under her view.

Kindle the flame, let love's fire soar,
'Burning thy love' forevermore.

No more shall the loser weep,
For in the finder's hands, it's theirs to
keep.

Wonder wall

A touch, indelible, never to fade,
A need, deep-seated, in my heart laid.

From the ashes of the past, you began,
Easily lifting the heart that ran.

A bird grounded, pain as wings
widespread,

You taught flight, ignoring the tangled
threads.

In the madness of gentle starlit nights,
We nestled close, city lights our sights.

Our feelings, like vines, grew strong and
wild,
Fuelled by conversations, miles compiled.

Now, in your presence, a soothing balm,
I let my guardian angels drink in calm.

This inescapable, irresistible pull,
Reignites the fire, burning deep and full.
My mind wanders in constant reminisce,
Ever since it was graced by your essence.

Captivated by the tempest in your gaze,
Our lips a perfect symphony, a
harmonious maze.

Songs and poetry falter in their quest,
Unable to capture what in you is best.

Your gravity, a force that draws me near,

Reveals a world worth seeing, crystal
clear.

This madness, inexplicable, profound,
Feels like a past life, in mystery bound.

Hello, my tomorrow, my awakening light,
Rouse me from sorrow, bring dawn to my
night.

Out in the cosmos, where dreams
intertwine,
Your place is beside me, eternally mine.

We've left Earth's embrace, its tethering
hold,
Embarking on adventures, bold and
untold.

With smiles as our compass, our hearts as
our guide,
On winds of fate, together we ride.

Like the finest wine, timeless and divine,
You are, unequivocally, eternally mine.

Just You, Just Me

Let's chase the stars,
One by one,
Across the endless galaxies' span.

Let's breathe life into dreams,
One by one,
In a castle where magic gleams.

Together, hand in hand,

Heart to heart,
Under heavenly clouds, on this land.

In this world, all we need is us,
Just you, just me,
In our bond, so wondrous.

By my side, stay ever near!

Let's reclaim the moments,
Once more rewind,
Journey back, where memories align.

Starting anew, our play of life,
Shining bright, unburdened by strife.

Together, hand in hand,
In unity's stand.

No tears to shed,
No fears to dread,

All we need is us,
Just you, just me,
In our love, we trust.

Let's liberate ourselves,
One by one,
From the chains that silence our tales.

Opening our eyes,
One by one,
To a vision that defies.

In kindness forever bind,
In love, blissfully blind.

It's just us we need,
Just you, just me,
In this journey, we lead.

Through the years, near or far,
Our bond will shine like a star.

Just you and me,
In this dance of destiny.

The Titanic

Submerge me,
Let me descend to the sea's somber
depths,
To a realm distant, detached,
Far away, far away.

In my descent,
I raise a voice, echoing,
A plea to be heard,

Far away, far away.

I am the Titanic,
Destined to sink,
Yet in your memories, eternally linked.

I am the Titanic,
Bound to fracture,
Yet from your heart, I'll never detach.

I am the Titanic,
Condemned to the cold,
But my soul, to you, will forever hold.
The saga continues,
With memories forged,
Stretching towards you,
Far away, far away.

In spirit, by your side,
In the end, our fates allied.
Had I lived, our hands entwined,
Far away, far away.

I am the Titanic,
Inevitably to submerge,
Yet in your thoughts, I'll always emerge.

I am the Titanic,
Though I may shatter,
My essence from your heart, won't scatter.

I am the Titanic,
Though encased in ice,
My soul's caress, eternally nice.

Unwilling to bid farewell,
I am the Titanic – a story to tell.

Language of the Angels

Dawn breaks,
A canvas of morning sun,
Stars dissolve in the day begun.
Birdsong fills the air, a symphonic view,
I awaken to a world anew.

Buttons clasped, tie knotted tight,

Guitar in hand, I step into the light.
Through the doorway, into life's embrace,
I wander along the sea's vast space.

Golden sun above, yet it rains,
A downpour of joy, of ecstatic pains.
Strange, this return to known shores,
On the brink of the unknown, heart's
unopened doors.

In this world's madness, colour fades
away,
A pretence to shield the hurt at bay.
Alone, with wounds concealed,
In my heart's chamber, quietly sealed.

Above, the sky burns, an endless flame,
Though things end, their essence remains
the same.
The days spent, a lifetime given,
To you, a dedication, endlessly driven.

Eyes closed, I hear the symphonies play,
Echoes of memories, in harmonious array.
Hard to greet farewell with a welcoming
smile,

When goodbye means losing, mile after
mile.

Lost, what I could never claim,
Washed away, like a forgotten name.
When my final moment draws near,
Let memories of me gently disappear.

Someday, I'll ascend, take flight,
A journey beyond the stars, into the night.

Release me to the universe's grand flow,
I hear them now – the angels' language,
soft and low.

Old Soul, New Heart

In a tale of yore, under weeping skies,
I stood, a war's echo in my cries.

Then you appeared, a beacon so bright,
Took my hand, and in darkness, you were
my light.

Should lightning strike, right through my
core,
Beside me, you'd shine, my celestial lore.

You awakened a truth, deep within,
With you, a heart begins.

You taught me courage, in the face of
despair,
With you, the world's fall, I can bear.

Grant me a heart,
One that echoes your own,
A rhythm for you, in every tone.

Gift me moments, a lyrical spree,
In your heartbeat, let my own be free.

With this heart, I run, I soar,
No looking back, now and forevermore.
Beneath the sky, where day greets night,
I might glimpse the moon, in the morning
light.

A dreamer I am, with a soul aged in time,

Your name etched in this heart, in broken
rhyme.

If pain were to come, a dagger's deep
thrust,
In your presence, in my vows, I trust.

You've given me a heart,
A vibrant, beating start.

You've shown me love, in its truest art.

Grant me a heart,
A reflection of yours,
In its rhythm, a love that endures.

Through mistral winds, I am led,
To your gentle touch, where my fears
shed.

I gaze at mountains, at heaven's gate,
There you are, in love, I await.

The sea whispers secrets, a siren's song,
Telling of your longing, where I belong.

I journey to return my heart to you,
In your embrace, our love anew.
If magic is real, let it be shown,
In the heart I give, forever your own.

In The Fountain of Miracles

Birds call in the dawn's embrace,
I find myself falling,
Into love, into grace,
Like a summer morning's face.

It shines, radiant and bright,

My love, my guiding light.
Spring whispers its arrival near,
Here I stand, love's volunteer.

The wind carries a song, a melody of
thought,
This love, this wonder, cannot be bought.

In the fountain of miracles, where dreams
take flight,
Let's dwell in a fairy tale, bathed in
magic's light.
Far from the world we left behind,
In this realm, our hearts entwined.

Even in darkness, my heart you'll see,
Glowing, radiant, forever free.
Birds sing of love's sweet decree,
As a summer morning, my love is free.
Spring's promise, tender and near,
In its bloom, I am here, ever clear.

Angels watch over us, in their light we
bask,
Guarding our love, an unspoken task.
I'll keep you close, never out of sight,

In this love, bathed in eternal light.

Join me on this journey, pure and true,
Hand in hand, in a world anew.
You are the light that guides my way,
In your eyes, my forever day.

In this fountain of miracles, where dreams
are alive,
Our love, a testament, will forever thrive.

Birds herald our love's sweet song,
In this summer morning, where we
belong.
Spring nears, with promises to give,
In this love, in this moment, we truly live.

Psychedelia

Love's Voyage:
In ordinary days, I met your gaze,
You, a radiant sun in life's mundane haze.
Your heartbeat's thunder, in my soul did
play,
Could this be love? I dared to hope and
pray.
Deep in your eyes, a flame forever lit,
In that mesmerizing glow, my heart was
hit.
I reached for stars in the endless night,
To take you with me, felt so right.

A Meeting of Hearts:
The day you graced my world with grace,
In your presence, confusion I'd embrace.
Is it a dream or fate's tender wish?
In my thoughts of you, my heart would
swish.
Your essence, unique, I couldn't decipher,
Yet, I sensed a love that might linger.
People change, growing far apart,
But the emotions we share, a work of art.
A Proposal of Love:
In the book of life, a page I sought,
A chapter of love, with you, I thought.
For this moment, I've yearned so long,
Let our love sing, like a beautiful song.
Together, let's fly in the sun's embrace,
In the azure sky, our hearts find their
place.
Dancing in nature's embrace so sweet,
Hand in hand, our love's heartbeat.

A Farewell Unsaid:
Words unspoken, locked inside,
From your eyes, I chose to hide.
Speechless, I run from what's true,

My heart aches, yet I leave, it's what I'll
do.
It hurts, for it's you, my dear,
Letting go brings a silent tear.
Release me from these bonds, let me go,
Will you, my love, in silence, so?

The Melodrama of Love:
Walking past, we meet and part,
Two souls connected from the heart.
In the night's embrace, questions arise,
Arms around, a whispered sigh.
Look into your heart, do you see me
there?
In your mind, do you think of us, do you
dare?
Vanishing in echoes, my dream in the
night,
One heart, one love, our guiding light.

Together, forever:
Close my eyes, I see your radiant light,
Guiding me through the darkest night.
Your love, a path for my heart to follow,
Together, we fly, like birds in the swallow.
Let colors fill the endless sky,

No obstacles shall make us say goodbye.
Your smile, your touch, your love so true,
Till the end of time, I'll be with you.
In this poem, the story of love unfolds,
Two hearts, once separate, now together,
their tale holds.
Through life's ups and downs, they find
their way,
In love's embrace, forever they'll stay.

A Letter to My Princess

To,
You

From,
Me

Dearest,

Bathed in fireflies' gentle hue,
Dream, for my thoughts cradle you.

As stars sprinkle the night's embrace,
My heart mirrors their radiant grace.

Through twilight's whisper, soft and light,
Your spirit shines, eternally bright.

In slumber's cocoon, safe you'll dwell,
Guarded by love's enduring spell.

And as the moon watches from above,
Know you're cherished, with boundless love.
Rest now, under the celestial sight,
Forever yours, your faithful knight.

Just Remember, I Love You

In the velvet night,
We dance, veiled in mystery's light,
With clouds like magic spun,
Under a sky shared by two radiant ones.

A comet streaks in fiery flight,
The Milky Way, a luminous stripe,
Stars burst forth in a vibrant glow,
Surrounding dreams that in my essence
flow.

From the depths of my mind, they rise,
In this moment, under celestial skies.

I cast my heart into the fray,
Let my pulse skip and sway,
Step back, into the shadow's play,
But in your memory, these words stay:
"I love you," I fervently convey.

Teach me to breathe, in this dance anew,
Challenge my steps, under skies so blue,
Guide me to redemption's dawn,
Let me chase the thunderous morn,
Ease the wind that on me preys,
You, the muse of my days.

I throw my heart, let it soar,
Feel my rhythm skip once more,
Walk into the night's embrace,
Yet remember, love's eternal trace.

Reclaim my life, timeless and true,
Let time heal wounds, old and new,
I'll share your tears, bear your fears,
In this confession, my love appears.

Days crystallized in memory's hue,
Now I stand, bathed in moonlight's dew.

Should angels weep, I'll heed their call,
On the road ahead, I won't fall.

My heart thrown, my beat skipped,
In shadows' arms, I'm gently gripped,
Walk away, into the night's deep blue,
But always remember, "I love you."

Happily, Ever After

Across a thousand miles I've raced,
In search of love, unseen, untraced.

Here I stand, to uncover love's embrace,
To touch your hand, with feather's grace.

Together, let's ascend into the sky,
In this journey where dreams never die.

My heart, stolen by a dream so new,
Yearns for the moment I find you.

Long have I sought your gaze,
Through countless nights and days.

Halt the slaughter of dreams so bright,
Cease the quelling of fanciful flight.

Spread your wings, in belief soar high,
Join me in the boundless sky.

To a realm where dreams weave our fate,
Happily Ever After, at love's ornate gate.
I've glimpsed the girl I've longed to meet,
Chasing her shadow, fleeting and fleet.
I vow to her, in words renewed,
Her dreams are hers, never to be subdued.

She stands on fantasy's precipice, bold,
In a story of magic, waiting to be told.

It's the way of love, wild and free,
The way it is, the way it should be.

Dare to love, take the leap,
Reclaim the dreams you're meant to keep.

End the demise of dreams so grand,
End the stifling of fantasy's land.

Act II: Loss and Despair

The Burden of
My Heart

"In the quiet of a world asleep,
A lost soul wandered, lone and deep.

Till it found an empty heart, still and
stark,
And without a reason, kindled a spark.

Fate stood as their foe, love as their ally,
In their silent world, no need for a lie.

Secrets whispered under the moon's
gentle care,
In the knowing eyes, a bond rare.

A fire ignited between you and me,
Laughter soaring high, wild, and free.

Memories flood in, a joyful tide,
In those moments, fears would subside.

The empty heart yearned to keep the
guest near,
Yet life's design, ever complex, ever
austere.

As fate's hand drew close, time's sands
thin,
Pain surfaced, a poignant sting within.

Though winds of change may drive us
apart,

A lost soul has found refuge in an empty
heart.
The burden I bear, the weight that is true,
Is the enduring presence of you."

The Soul taker

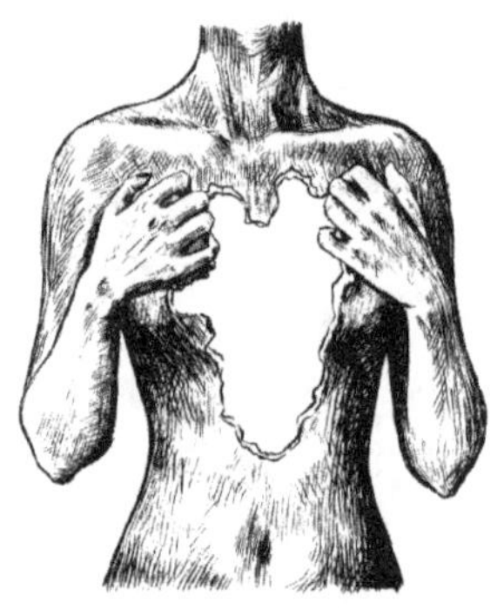

In this realm, I find my solace,
Not alone, in this embrace, I face.

Free from gravity's binding chain,
This surreal effect, is it my gain?
Am I nearing the end, the final bend?
Is this all that's left to defend,
Of this human state, so frail and spent?
Oh, Soul taker, claim my soul's ascent.

Dear Soul taker,
Whisk my soul away.

Dear Soul taker,
Relieve me of this fray.

No desire left to delay.

Before I depart,
Let's strike a pact, an art.
One final night in this realm of spite,
In this world of sin, where shadows alight.
In this illusion, pain was my only
companion.

Dear Soul taker,
Grant my soul its liberation.

Dear Soul taker,
End this earthly probation.

Longing no more for continuation.

Before I fade,
My heart's shadows, unswayed.

Confessions cut, no guise, no deception,
I can't feign, let fate make its interception.
Just a man, with a mind encased,
In a box of memories, interlaced.

Dear Soul taker,
Eclipse my soul with your wake.

Dear Soul taker,
This mortal coil, forsake.

I yearn not for another dawn to break.
My journey halted, the castle afar,
Confronting past scars, a never-ending
war.
In the mirror, my mourning eyes stare,
No longer able to bear,
This life of chains, this mournful fare.

Dear Soul taker,
Relieve me from this despair.

Dear Soul taker,
Hear my final prayer.

From this sorrow, I seek repair.

As I lay down,
In this lifeless town,
I dream of a realm beyond mortal crown.

In heaven's eye, with tears that dry,
Where time stands still, under an eternal
sky.
In fire's ring, my sins unshared,
In Soul taker's grace, my soul bared.

Dear Soul taker,
Now, take me, I've dared.
Dear Soul taker,
My sunshine, I've shared.

For release, I am prepared.

Fallen Feathers

Misunderstood, I stand,
Far from noble truths' land.
Grounded still, with both feet firm,
Yearning to reverse the turn.

Devils circle as I seek,
No heavenly gates for the meek.

In the end,

Rebirth is not my friend.

I'm no seraph, no haloed glow,
Saintliness, I cannot show.

A bird, yet bound to earth,
Wings clipped, denying flight's birth.

No angel, no saintly guise,
A fish, yet the water I defy.

Not blinded eternally,
I seek wisdom, a key to be free.

There's a place for me here,
Your path yours, mine clear.

In love's pursuit, I'll delve,
Memories behind my eyes, shelved.

I may stumble, may fade from view,
Chasing small joys, discoveries anew.

No halo crowns my head,
Yet in prayer, my thoughts are led.
The world, a gift, in my sight,

Unchanging, in day and night.

A legacy of meaning, I aspire to leave,
Wild at heart, in wonderland I weave.
A journey long, a path untrod,

No angel, no saint, just flawed.

A bird, yet in flight restrained,
A fish, yet from swimming abstained.

In Search of Salvation

Aboard this grand starship, I soar,
Flying far, fast, with a heart unmoored.
Sober in thought, through the cosmos I breach,
Breaking barriers, to distant stars I reach.
In the vast unknown, I find my quest,
Counting moments, in celestial zest.

Torn by forces, gravity's relentless pull,

In a faceless void, yet my heart is full.

Amidst black hole's spin, one vision stays
true,
Your face, a guiding light, in the cosmic
blue.

I am but an atom,
Drifting, desperate, alone,
Clinging to a single truth I've known:
You.

In this tranquil expanse,
Peace fragments me, piece by piece.
I ponder, I fear, in my celestial lease.

What pains more in this cosmic tide?
Leaving all behind in my astral ride,

Or being the one left, as everything fades,
In the relentless march of time's parades?

Trapped between memories orbiting you,
And forging new ones, while old haunts
accrue.

This isn't about when our paths will align,
But if.
If I'll breathe the air that you've breathed,
Share molecules in space, seamlessly
sheathed.
If I'll gaze into the blackness of your eyes,
Feel your touch, my heart's prize.

Once, we gazed at the sky, dreaming our
place.
Now, amidst the stars, I realize my space.
It's beside you, yet each cosmic display,
Each sun, each star, lights my way.

They whisper of hope, of dawn's gentle
hue,
Assuring me, through darkness, I'll find
you.

Yes, I will unravel the secrets of space,
Challenge fate, our doomed destiny erase.

My love, timeless, in every particle spun,
In the vast universe, under every sun.

My quest for salvation spans the celestial
sphere,
But know this, my dearest, my salvation is
here.

In you, my love, my constant, my true,
In the vast, starry expanse, it's always
been you.

Nosferatu

In earthly guise, the devil, and his kin
tread,
I pray our paths never be led.

In this creature, lessons lurk, dark and
deep,
Oh, how I yearn for you, my potential feast
to keep.

Boundless as science and fiction's domain,
So is my addiction, my unspoken bane.

My longing for you, ineffable, intense,
Thoughts of you, bordering on the
immense.

Beneath lands, lost, beyond the forest's
edge,
I implore, keep your distance, make a
pledge.

Blood, the embodiment of my sorrowful
tears,
In this madness, I am ensnared for years.

A being immune to death's embrace,
Vowing to erase every human trace.
Once a sovereign of the nocturnal sphere,
Now, my might has vanished,
disappeared.

In death's shadows, with Nosferatu, I
roam,
Bonded with you, in this eternal gloom.
Aye, Dracula, beyond divine grace, I dwell,

Lifeless,
Soulless,
Despised,
Dreaded,
Yet, in existence, I remain,
Forever craving the living's vein.

Since You Went Away

In the cloak of night,
The stars have dimmed their light,
My guiding beacon, once so bright,
Now lost to sight.

Their lustre waned,
Since you're no longer claimed,

In my heart, I hope you've gained,
Peace, unashamed.

They dwindle, night by night,
As you drifted from my sight,
This day, bereft of light,
Is my plight.

The sky, no longer a vibrant hue,
Clueless, I'm lost without you,
My time, like morning dew,
Fades from view.

This longing stretches, long and deep,
As I pen this song, in solitude, I weep,
Wishing you strength, a promise to keep,
In memories we steep.

Tears linger, unshed, unspoken,
Since the day our bond was broken,
The reason, a mystery, a token,
Of love unspoken.

Since you went away,
My world's turned an endless gray,
A void where my heart used to sway,

Since you went away.

Since you went away,
In a silent, echoing fray,
A whisper of the love that lay,
Since you went away.

Adieu To You

Time's wheel spins, relentless, true,
This is the feeling, bitter and blue.
We yearn to rewind, to moments anew,
To speak of love and needs, through and
through,
To express our hate yet confess our
missing you.

Life's path is uncertain, its destination
unclear,
The thought of never seeing you again, my
deepest fear.
You wiped away my tears, year after year,
In life's fragility, you taught me to
persevere.

We played, we screamed, our spirits free,
Never imagining parting ways, never
foreseeing the decree.
We gazed at the skies, time fleeting by,
Blissfully ignorant, never questioning
why.

Farewell, a word so heavy, so hard to say,
Memories weigh us down, in their own
unique way.
My friend, in battles, you stood by me,
In laughter and tears, you set me free.
Your presence, a constant, a guiding key,
Until the end, you'll always be.

In every goodbye, there's a soul to miss,
Like the sun that sets, in the night's abyss.

But remember, it rises anew, with dawn's
kiss.
In every storm, seek the rainbow's bliss,
Spread your wings, in life's ceaseless quiz.

Heaven sent you, a journey to unfold,
The best days await, bright and bold.

When Angels Fall

Oh, when you smile,
It's like a spell divine,
The rainbow pales in comparison,
Yet in my eyes, you shine.

Oh, when tears grace your cheeks,
A spell you cast anew,

The ocean stirs in empathy,
But I'll stand steadfast, true.

My heart, unknowingly, reaches for you,
My eyes, unbidden, seek your view.

In your absence, the dawn loses its glow,
In dreams I linger, where love's embers
grow.
When angels fall, you beckon me too,
Unsure of all, but for you, I'll pursue.

How I wish I were the cause of your tears,
To know it wasn't me, is my deepest fear.
If it wasn't my doing that brought your
pain,
In that truth, let me fade, let me wane.

Confusion clouds, what is right, what is
wrong,
If you hold the key, to you I belong.
Illuminate my sight, let the truth be
shown,
In that revelation, let our paths be known.

To the truth, the unspoken, the unseen,

In your light, let me find what love may
mean.

62

Farewell My Queen

At this journey's final bend,
Where roads part and dreams extend.

With new horizons to explore,
And thoughts uncharted like before.

My heart, I lay at your feet, serene,

As I drift into the unseen.

Farewell, my queen, under night's
embrace,
To the skies, from this earthly place.

Farewell, my queen, in morning's light,
To the stars, in heaven's flight.

In these fleeting moments, know I'm near,
Before I vanish, into the ether clear.

Inside, complexities too vast to unveil,
No need for words, our bond will prevail.

Lessons etched deep within my core,
Your words, a guiding lore.

Time shall ease your sorrow's sway,
As I journey far away.

Farewell, my queen, in the cloak of night,
To celestial realms, out of sight.

Farewell, my queen, in dawn's tender
glow,
To heavenly heights, I must go.

In my departure, a silent plea,
Forgive my letting go, let me be free.

Why?

Why can't I close my eyes for good,
To miss the world's misunderstood?

Why can't I shred this pride of mine,
To mend bridges, in forgiveness find?

Why can't I silence my mind's loud roar,
To let my heart, and only it, soar?

Why can't I still this beating heart,
To be immune from pain's sharp dart?

Why can't I untether soul from flesh,
To let it wander, in freedom fresh?

Why can't I turn back time's swift hands,
To relive pasts, redo life's plans?

Why does the Divine instil in me,
Questions of its own reality?

Why can't I unravel every mystery,
If answers exist in life's vast library?
In pondering existence, in seeking truth,
I find the essence of my youth.
Yet in the asking and the quest,
Lies life's journey, its ultimate test.

My Last Wish

I yearn to race
Alongside the river's grace,

To soar high
With clouds in the sky.

I dream to yell
Atop mountains where eagles dwell,

To leap and reach
The heavens, within my speech.

I wish to roam
With the wind, my endless tome,

To dive and dwell
In ocean's secretive shell.

I long to sway
In the sun's golden ray,

To tread lightly
Upon a star, shining brightly.
I desire to sing
In harmony with birds on wing,

To embrace the wild,
In paradise, nature's child.

I aspire to challenge
My heart, in balance,

To weave tales
Of adventures that set gales.

I seek a game
With death, a fleeting flame,

To return with speed,
In life's relentless creed.

Indifferent to fear,
Uncaring of the tear,

I wish to live
This dream, with all I can give,

To do it all, once more,
In life's unending encore.

Act III: Legacy and Redemption

Remember Me

Remember me,
As the sculptor of your effigy,
Etched atop my heart, a legacy.

Recall me,
As one caught in a relentless tug,
Between the wisdom of mind and heart's
embrace snug.

Envision me,
On the precipice, where life and demise
align,
Balancing on the narrow bridge of time.

Close your eyes,
Let my memory softly rise.

As I tread away,
Leaving the sun to light another day,

Believe,
In your heart's chamber, I shall forever
weave.
Remember me.

Recall my spirit,
In dreams, my presence visit.
Bid farewell,
Let go, but in your thoughts, let my
essence dwell.

Remember me,
In the undying beat of my heart, eternally
free.

Burn Your Tears

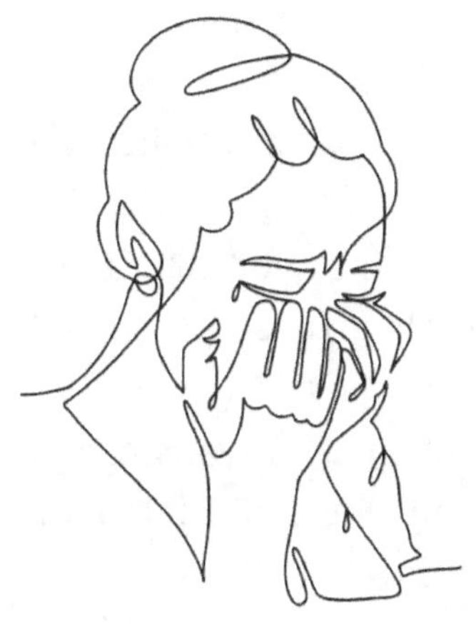

Abandon the shadows,
Of moonless, starless nights,
Step away from the darkened realms,
Of your heart's internal fights.

Don't just gaze at the sky,
Your past - a whisper, a sigh.

We are destined for more than mere
existence,
Break free from the chains of inner
resistance.

Beyond this feeling, there's a world to
embrace,
Push beyond limits, join life's relentless
race.
A destiny awaits, vibrant and inviting,
With every heartbeat, our spirit's writing.

Seize the chance for transformation,
You have one life, make it a bold
declaration.
Be the architect of your dreams,
Unfurl your wings, let go of past screams.

Though bent and scarred, remain
unbroken,
Keep your eyes wide open.

There's more to witness, more to achieve,
Embrace your dream, in yourself believe.
What you envision, you can become,
In life's symphony, be the beating drum.

Every second is precious, a priceless
sound,
Every minute, an opportunity profound.

Let each day echo with your song's
melody,
Shape the world with your harmony.

Try again, overturn the night,
Chase your dreams, embrace the light.
Join me here, where fears are spurned,
Where tears are flames, forever burned.

Yesterday's shadows, let them fade,
History's written, but today's still played.

This game of life is far from done,
It's more than battles lost or won.

Just one life, a singular story,
No promised afterlife, no secondary glory.
Embrace the now, live with passion,
Burn your tears, in a blaze of action.

Eternal

Hey you,
Girl in the crimson hue,
Missed your bus, it's true,
But don't let it trouble you.

Hey you,
Boy with the guitar's charm,
Your train's departed, don't be alarmed.

And you,
People under the streetlight's glow,
Looking upwards, your prayers in tow,
They may not cease, but let them flow.

Hoping doesn't harm, it's a vigilant eye,
Believing someone's watching from the
sky.
But cease your search, don't always vie,
Heroes don't emerge in every battle cry.
Consider the sacrifices, since your dawn,
In fading times, their worth drawn.

Oh, we dwell in a world, isolated and cold,
A narrative, from old times, we've been
told.

Cease overthinking, it leads to despair,
Yet in giving up, find no solace there.
Nurture growth, let resilience flare,
Promises we make, in depth, we care.

Your contribution, no matter small or
grand,

Remember, you're part of a fable, a story grand.
We all partake in this life's game,
Seeking fame, a fleeting flame.

Everyone craves the rush, the thrill,
Yet only a few hold the strength, the will.

Be steadfast, immovable in strife,
Life, though sturdy, is rife.
Break free, embrace the transient ride,
But in your heart, let the spirit reside.

Tree of Immortality

In lands where wisdom's tree does grow,
A man once tread, his pace was slow.
To Philos came, with hope to know,
The secrets deep, where immortals go.

"Why seek ye such a fate?" inquired he,
Philos, whose eyes could worlds foresee.
"A thirst for knowledge, love's decree,
To live, to love, eternally."

"But what of paths that heavens show,
Would thou not rather those to follow?"
"Who dreams of heaven's fleeting glow,
When earth's immortal roots can grow?"

Philos, in silence, weighed the cost,
Of lives forever, never lost.
"Love's open heart may guide thee most,
Belief and courage, thy only host.

Yet, herein lies the twist, the bend,
The journey's start, not just its end.
Immortality for soul, I lend,
But flesh and bone, to earth must tend."

Disheartened, the man turned away,
His quest for eternal day,
Left unanswered, in dismay,
Philos sighed as he would say:

"Some truths in life, through living,
shown,
Are better felt than fully known.
For what is endlessly sought and pried,
In simple moments, often hides."

To his servant, wise words were cast,
"Experiences, not explanations, last.
In the search for life, unbound and vast,
It's the journey, not the end, that's
grasped.

Halle Halle

In the shroud of night, I roam,
Wondering, wandering, in the gloom.
In every corner, every shadow's throw,
I see you, in the moon's soft glow.

Here's a melody, a beacon bright,
To lift you up, reignite your fight.
Leap back into life's circling game,

Where each round is never quite the
same.

Should they desert you in night's cold
grasp,
Hold on, let your resolve tightly clasp.

If they dare to steal your soul's vibrant
hue,
Stand firm, never let your spirit rue.

Oh, please, let not tears fall,
Let oceans calm, at your beck and call.

Step away from shadows' silent screen,
Embrace the world, lush and green.

The world, with its trials, spins on,
Play your part with heart, until dawn.

Let your actions speak, your path define,
In the court of life, let your truth shine.

In the end, the puzzle will find its fit,
The pieces aligning, bit by bit.

Behold life's spectrum, vivid and bright,
Let clarity's beam fill your sight.

The spirit, undying, forever flies,
Hope, unyielding, in the skies.

So, if within your power it lies,
Restore faith, let it rise.

Illuminate the night, dispel the dark,
With a single, resilient, eternal spark.

I Am Here

Throughout my days, a ceaseless quest,
I've traversed many roads, no time to rest.
Thoughts spinning wildly in my mind,
I gaze upwards, answers to find.

Tonight, a pivotal moment in time,
I ponder, if leaving it all behind,
Would ease the whirlwind in my mind?

This hush within silence, unfamiliar yet
clear,
Perhaps more tales await, my heart to
steer.
Where to next? The path unclear.

Yet, as I stumble, as I fall,
I know I'll rise, stand tall.
Life's pushes, its relentless trial,
But I'll soar, cross the celestial mile,
Shedding my scars, embracing the stars.

Open your eyes, see me thrive,
Alive, reborn, in this life's dive.

The world may try to dim our spark,
But I hold fast to fairy tales in the dark.
Listen with your heart, not just your ear,
Believe in the magic, crystal clear.
Someday, my dear ones will hear.
The melodies I cherish, bringing them
near,
Guiding them to find their path, sincere.

Until that day, here I stand,

Unwavering, with an outstretched hand.

I will not stray, I will not flee,
In the pursuit of what can be.
Let's strive together, rise anew,
Breaking chains, our strength true.

Let's soar on wings unclipped, unbound,
Until our purpose is found.

This is who I am, untamed, unchained,
In the place I belong, uncontained.
A life pulsing to my heart's beat,
Awaiting me, a journey complete.

With wings outspread, in belief, we'll soar,
Together, into folklore.

To the world where dreams and love intertwine,
Happily, Ever After, where stars align.

Two Roads Diverged

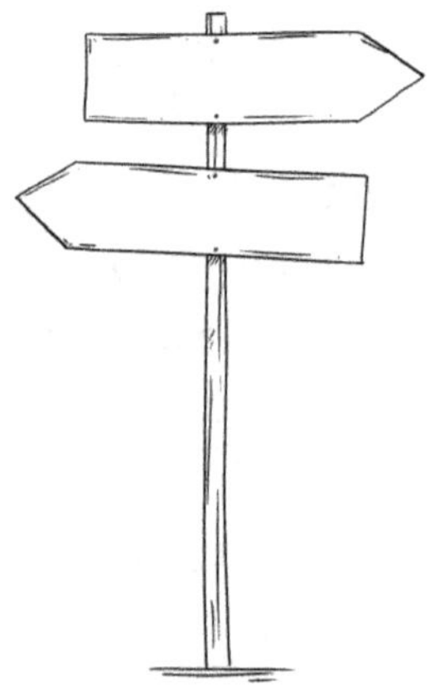

In this vast world, I stand and find,
I'm like the traveller, with a choice in
mind.
Two roads diverged in a yellow wood,
Each path distinct, as before them I stood.

One road, with its twists and bends,

Curves out of sight, where the unknown
extends.
The other, bathed in inviting light,
Promises a journey both clear and bright.

These two paths, they made me ponder,
Reflecting on the way I wander.

In choosing my path, I must be true,
For this journey is mine, through and
through.
Down the less travelled road I stride,
Leaving the common path aside,
Hoping the choice, I make today,
Brings fulfilment, not dismay.

Emotions aside, a decision made,
Where destiny's hand is gently laid.

The road I walk, steep though it may
appear,
I'll climb with resolve, conquering fear.
This uphill trek, not as daunting as it
seems,
I march onward, pursuing my dreams.

And one day, I'll look back, under the
sun's gold ray,
In the fields of success, where I'll lay my
hay.

I chose the road less travelled by,
And since then, regrets have passed me
by.
This road, my choice, uniquely mine,
Has shaped my life, in its own design.

Wings of Bravery

Those unseeing with eyes,
Perceive with hearts that never lie.
Those silent, without voice,
Speak volumes, with eyes that rejoice.

Those who in silence dwell,
Hear nature's whispers, clear as a bell.

Those graced with challenges, each day,
Wage battles with spirit, bold and gay.

Life, a tapestry of myth and enigma,
Demands strength, in its every stigma.
Pursue your dreams, with courage take flight,
For wings of bravery soar to great heights.

The Sun is Set for You

In the dawn's embrace, a stunning sight,
A surprise in the sunrise, so bright.

A dream in the night, worth its keep,
In the realm of stars, where thoughts leap.

A ray of light in your gaze, a spark,

Igniting fire in the dark.

A touch, unfelt, yet deeply known,
In the mind's expanse, silently shown.

A promise of a better morrow,
With you, free from sorrow.

I see the hues of a butterfly, vivid and true,
On the wings of your being, in every hue.

Your name, a rhythmic beat within my
heart,
In every pulse, a vital part.
My heart, with every beat, echoes your
name,
With you, life's not the same.

If I could, if I knew,
Turn back time, my actions I'd review,
I'd guard you close, never let you stray,
From the dreams where you forever stay.

In the quiet of the night, under starlit
skies,
I hope you feel, without disguise,

The depth of emotions, true and pure,
In love's embrace, forever sure.

For better or worse, to love, commit,
With every fibre, every bit.

The sun ascends, greeting your smile,
Warming hearts, across every mile.

May it soften your heart, once like stone,
With warmth that you've never known.

The sun sets, but for you, it stays,
In love's eternal, unending blaze,
Always and forever, for you it glows,
In the dance of light, love forever shows.

God - The Artist

Dear Human,

Why flee from rain's tender embrace,
When in its absence, you seek its grace?

Why shy away from the sun's warm kiss,
Yet in darkness, its light you miss?

Why reach for distant galaxies so far,

When unity on Earth remains ajar?

Why withhold a comforting shoulder to
share,
Yet long for support, when in despair?

Why wander, lost in life's vast maze,
Yet yearn for someone to find you in the
haze?

Why restrain the tears that yearn to flow,
When unburdening your heart is what
you know?

Why pursue paths that led astray,
Knowing right from wrong, yet still sway?

Why run from truths you cannot hide,
Memories, ever present, by your side?

Cease the endless quest for reasons to
love,
Open your heart to the skies above.

Embrace love, boundless and free,

For every soul, for you and me.

Love not merely for the divine sway,
Or judgment on life's final day.

Not just for love, unconditional and pure,
But for the artistry, timeless and sure.

For He is the artist, unparalleled,
profound,
In His creation, beauty and wonder
abound.

He crafted you, unique in every way,
A masterpiece, in this world's grand
display.

Why Do I Write?

Cloaked in invisibility, I wander,
Alone amidst a crowd's ponder.

Hearing cries masked by laughter's guise,
Attuned to whispers that cut and chastise.

In the sun's glare, darkness shrouds,
A life less fun, hidden in clouds.

A man of regrets, memories steadfast,
Clinging to moments, shadows of the past.

Emotions locked within, key thrown away,
Hidden from view, in my heart's quiet bay.

Rather than don a mask, live a lie,
I'd embrace the earth, let the world pass
by.

Directionless, I drift, lost in thought,
The future uncertain, the past a knot.

Pondering,

Am I mistaken in my claim of strength?
Is resilience just a dream at length?
Am I the curse amidst the blessed?
Spreading gloom, never at rest.

A bottle brimming with sorrow, filled to
the brim,
My will alone keeps me from growing
dim.

Yearning for a chance to lament with
another,
A tune to transform, a new path to
uncover.

Why do I write?

Is it a surrender, a battle lost in the night?
Or is it my power, a way I show my might?

Epilogue: A Call to Unwritten Journey

In the gentle embrace of the final page, as the whispers of "Unwritten: The Poems That Never Were" fade into the quietude of reflection, a singular truth emerges from the tapestry of thoughts we've explored together: the narrative of life, with its boundless potential for creation, remains ever incomplete, perpetually unwritten. This realization, far from being a source of despair, is a beacon of unbridled hope and infinite possibility.

As the architect of your own existence, you stand at the precipice of countless untold stories, each waiting for the courage of your voice to bring them into being. The invitation extended through these pages is not merely to ponder the abstract beauty of the stories left untold but to actively engage in the art of their creation. To pen down the words that tremble at the edge of thought, to voice the sentiments that lurk in the shadow of silence, is to partake in a profound act of liberation and self-discovery.

The journey of life, with its myriad paths and unforeseen detours, offers few guarantees save for the certainty of its end. In the face of this inevitable conclusion, the choice remains ours: to leave the canvas of our existence rich with the strokes of expressed thoughts and felt emotions, or to depart with the palette of our soul still full, the potential of our unwritten words and unsaid love lingering as the silent testimony of what could have been.

Let this epilogue serve not as a conclusion, but as a departure point for a journey inward, toward the heart of your own story. Embrace the chaos, the uncertainty, and the sheer beauty of the unwritten. Find peace in the realization that closure is a myth, and every end is but a doorway to new beginnings. Celebrate the courage that resides within you, for it is the compass that will guide you through the uncharted territories of your soul.

As "Unwritten: The Poems That Never Were" closes, let it mark the opening of your heart to the possibilities that lie within the silence, the gaps, and the pauses of your life. Write, speak, and live with the fullness of your being, unafraid of the imperfections and unfinished symphonies that define the human condition. For it is within these spaces that we find our true selves, and it is here, in the courage to confront the unwritten, that the poetry of life truly resides.

In the end, may we all find the strength to leave behind a legacy not of regrets, but of stories bravely told, of words fearlessly spoken, and of lives lived with an unyielding commitment to the beauty of the unfinished. Let us step forward with the knowledge that, within us, lies the power to illuminate the dark with the light of our unwritten words.

www.ingramcontent.com/pod-product-compliance
Lightning Source LLC
La Vergne TN
LVHW050909200726
843508LV00011B/2159